Discover
ENGLISH

Starter

Workbook

with CD-ROM

FIONA BEDDALL

What's Your Name?

Introductions

1 Order the dialogue.

- [ ] **a Jenny** My name's Jenny.
- [ ] **b Matt** Nice to meet you, Jenny.
- [1] **c Jenny** Hello.
- [ ] **d Jenny** Nice to meet you too.
- [ ] **e Matt** Hi! I'm Matt. What's your name?

2 Order the sentences.

Dracula Hi!

Tarzan Hello.

Dracula name   What's   your   ?

   1 *What's your name?*

Tarzan name's   Tarzan   My   .

   2 _____ .

   your   What's   name   ?

   3 _____ ?

Dracula Dracula   name's   My   .

   4 _____ .

Tarzan Nice   Dracula   to meet you   .

   5 _____ , _____ .

Dracula to meet you   Nice   too   .

   6 _____ .

The alphabet

3 Say the letters. Put them in the correct group.

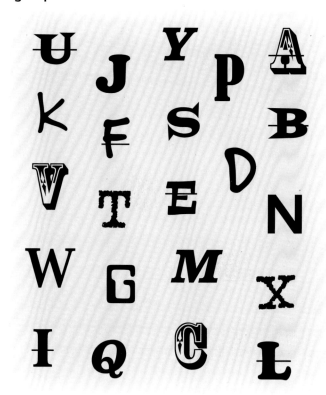

B E	F L	A	I	U

4 Circle the odd letter out. Complete the sentence with the circled letters.

1 A J Ⓔ K
2 D N E C
3 G N M S
4 U W Q L
5 I F L X
6 B T V S
7 G P H V

E _____ is cool!

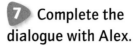

Puzzle Zone

5 Cross out the letters that rhyme with *me*. What is Sophie saying?

_____ !

e H D E i b p P
G C V T d V g

6 Write the question.

howdoyouspellsophie

_____ _____
_____ ?

S-O-P-H-I-E.

7 Complete the dialogue with Alex.

Alex What's your name?
You 1 *My name's* … _____ .
Alex How do you spell your name?
You 2 _____ .
Alex Thank you!
You 3 _____ ?
Alex My name's Alex.
You 4 _____ ?
Alex A-L-E-X.
You 5 _____ .

Talking Tips!

8 Complete the words.

A C _o_ __ e a __ __ h __ __ p!

B C __ __ l!

A Red And Blue Bag

Numbers 0–10

1 Write the missing letters. Match the words with the numbers.

0   1   2   3   4   5   6   7   8   9   10

_t_ wo
n __ __ e
t __ __ e __
s __ x
z __ r __
f __ v __
e __ __ h t
f __ __ r
s __ v __ __
__ e n
o __ e

2 Write the next number.

1 four, three, two, _one_
2 two, four, six, _____
3 one, three, five, _____
4 nine, eight, seven, _____
5 six, four, two, _____
6 zero, one, two, _____

My things

3 Circle the words. Match them with the pictures.

bagoboxapplebshirtoballpencilkpen

① ② ③ ④ ⑤ ⑥ ⑦

4 Look at the other letters in Exercise 3. Write the word and add the sticker.

b _____

Sticker

Colours

5 Match the word halves.

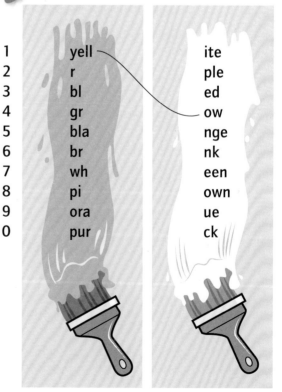

1 yell   ite
2 r   ple
3 bl   ed
4 gr   ow
5 bla   nge
6 br   nk
7 wh   een
8 pi   own
9 ora   ue
10 pur   ck

6 Complete the colour sums.

1 red + yellow = *orange*
2 red + white = _____
3 yellow + blue = _____
4 blue + red = _____

7 Colour the numbers and find the objects. Then answer the questions.

one = brown	six = pink
two = yellow	seven = red
three = white	eight = purple
four = blue	nine = orange
five = black	ten = green

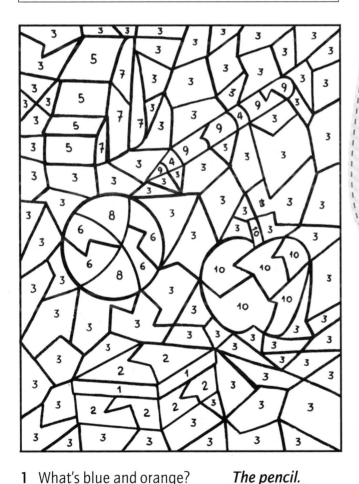

1 What's blue and orange?   *The pencil.*
2 What's brown and yellow?   _____
3 What's green?   _____
4 What's red and black?   _____
5 What's pink and purple?   _____

Puzzle Zone

8 Find the words in the chart. Write the questions and answer them.

0	1	2	3
phone	**black**	name	**your**
4	5	6	7
white	number	What's	**and**

1 six three two?
What's your name?
My name's… _____ .
2 six three zero five?
_____ ?
_____ .
3 six one seven four?
_____ ?
The _____ .

The Magic Mirror

Numbers 11–20

1 Complete the puzzle.

13▼
18► E I G H T E E N
11▼ 15►
19▼
20►
12►
17►
16►
14►

2 Write the numbers in the boxes and do the sums.

1 sixteen 16 + three 13 = nineteen 19
2 one ☐ + eleven ☐ = _____ ☐
3 thirteen ☐ + seven ☐ = _____ ☐
4 fifteen ☐ + five ☐ = _____ ☐
5 six ☐ + twelve ☐ = _____ ☐
6 fourteen ☐ + three ☐ = _____ ☐

3 Circle the odd word out.

1 seven   twenty   (bag)   fourteen
2 red   blue   green   twelve
3 black   eleven   red   brown
4 box   apple   book   purple
5 pink   yellow   dog   white
6 your   hi   hello   bye

Talking about age

4 Complete the dialogue. Use these words. Make the last sentence true for you.

~~How~~   you   I'm   old

You   Hi. ¹*How* old are
²_____ ?
Jo-Jo   ³_____ eleven.
How ⁴_____ are you?
You   I'm _____ .

5 Match the questions with the answers.

1 What's your name?
2 What's your phone number?
3 How old are you?

a It's cool!
b 264381.
c Nice to meet you too.
d My name's Oscar.

4 This is a magic mirror.
5 Nice to meet you.

b I'm ten.

1 Families

My Picture Dictionary

The family

1 Write the words in the correct box.

brother dad sister mum
granny granddad

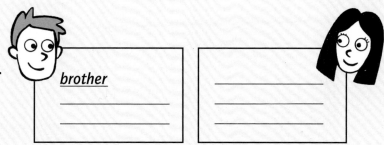

brother
_____
_____

_____
_____
_____

2 Label the picture with the words from Exercise 1.

1 brother

2 _____

3 _____

4 _____

5 _____

6 _____

BILLY
ZAC
LULU
JED
IZZY
JILLY
JESS
MILLY
FRED
ED

my words

Write about your family.

My family is my _____ , my _____ , _____ .

Discover **5** extra words. Go to page 71.

to be

1 ☆ Complete the sentences. Use these words.

> He ┼ She We It They

1

I am Alex.

2

_____ are Sophie and Matt.

3

_____ is Jenny.

4

_____ is my dad.

5

_____ are happy.

6

_____ is a ball.

2 ☆ Complete the text. Use with these words.

> It ┼ It I We He She

Hi. ¹*I* am Matt.
²_____ am with my family today.
³_____ are happy. This is my brother, Luke.
⁴_____ is thirteen. My granny is here too.
⁵_____ is with my dog. ⁶_____ is a big dog. ⁷_____ is brown and white.

3 ☆ Complete. Use *is*, *are* or *am*.

1 Hi! My name *is* Luke.
2 I _____ thirteen.
3 Matt _____ eleven.
4 We _____ brothers.
5 My mum and dad _____ Mike and Helen.
6 They _____ with my granny.

4 ☆☆ Circle the correct word.

Hi! ¹(**I**) / **She** am Becky. I ²**am** / **are** happy today. It ³**am** / **is** my birthday. ⁴**We** / **I** am with my brother and sisters. Joshua is my brother. ⁵**He** / **She** is thirteen. Lily, Grace and Saskia ⁶**are** / **they** my sisters. ⁷**They** / **She** are fifteen, eighteen and twenty. We ⁸**is** / **are** a big family!

Puzzle Zone

5 Look at the puzzle. Write sentences.

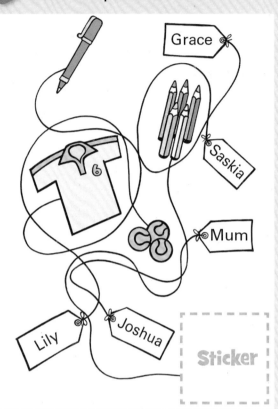

Grace

Saskia

Mum

Joshua

Lily

Sticker

1 *The pen is* from my sister Grace.
2 _____
   from my brother Joshua.
3 _____
   from my sister Saskia.
4 _____
   from my sister Lily.

6 Add the sticker and answer the question.

What's from my mum?
A _____

to be: contractions

6 ☆ Write the contractions.

1 I am   *I'm*
2 you are   _____
3 he is   _____
4 she is   _____
5 it is   _____
6 we are   _____
7 they are   _____

7 ☆☆ Complete the sentences.
Use contractions.

1 Hello. My name **'s** Lily.
2 I _____ with my sister, Becky.
3 She _____ ten today.
4 Saskia _____ here, and Grace too.
5 They _____ my sisters.
6 We _____ very happy!

Talking Tips!

8 Complete the sentences. Use these words in
the box. Match the pictures with the sentences.

Smile   ~~Cool~~   Come and help   Watch out

1 Look at the dog. *Cool*! D
2 Mum! _____ with this box!
3 Now, a photo! _____ !
4 The guitar! _____ !

Ⓐ

Ⓑ

Ⓒ

Ⓓ

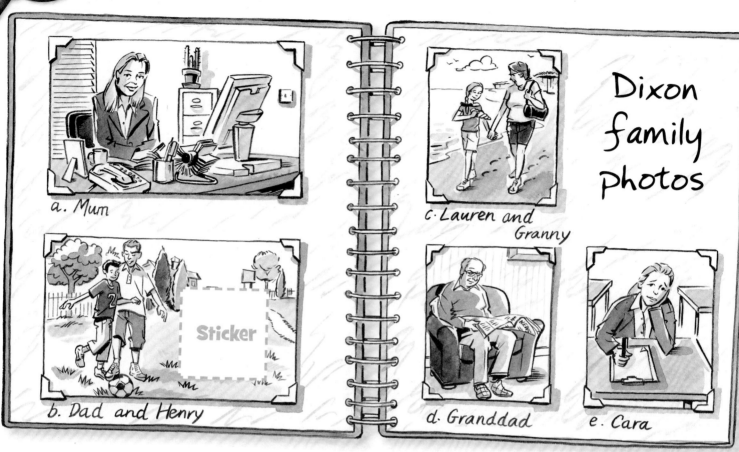

a. Mum

b. Dad and Henry

Dixon family photos

c. Lauren and Granny

d. Granddad

e. Cara

Places

1 Complete the words. Match them with the Dixon's family photos.

1 p _a_ _r_ k | _b_ |
2 b __ __ c h | |
3 w __ __ k | |
4 s __ __ o o __ | |
5 h __ m __ | |

2 Write the words from Exercise 1 in the correct box.

At the...	At...
park	

3 Complete the sentences about the Dixon family. Use *at* or *at the* and the words in Exercise 1. Add the sticker to picture b.

1 Dad and Henry are ***at the park*** .
2 Mum is _____ .
3 Lauren and Granny are _____ .
4 Granddad is _____ .
5 Cara is _____ .
6 Toby the dog is _____ with Dad and Henry.

4 Write four true sentences about you and your family. Use *at* or *at the*.

My sister is at school.

_____

_____

_____

_____

to be: negative

5 ☆ **Look at the Dixon family photos. Complete Cara's sentences. Who is it?**

> isn't (x4)   aren't (x2)   ~~'m not~~ (x2)

1 I **'m not** at the beach and I **'m not** happy.   *Cara*
2 She _____ with Granny and she _____ at school.   _____
3 They _____ at work and they _____ with Henry.   _____
4 He _____ with Dad and he _____ at the park.   _____

6 ☆ **Write the sentences. Do not use contractions.**

1 You aren't Henry.

   You are not Henry.

2 Henry isn't nineteen.

   _____

3 Lauren and Cara aren't brothers.

   _____

4 I'm not at the park.

   _____

7 ☆☆ **Read Henry's sentences about his family photos. Complete them with the correct form of *to be*, affirmative or negative.**

1 This **is** my mum. She _____ at home in this picture. She _____ at work.
2 In this picture, my granny _____ with my granddad. She _____ with my sister, Lauren. They _____ at the beach.
3 I _____ at school in this picture. I _____ with my dad. We _____ at the park.
4 My granddad _____ at home in this picture. He _____ at the beach with Lauren.
5 My sister Cara _____ in this picture. She _____ at the park. She _____ happy!

Puzzle Zone

8 **Where are they? Read and complete.**

Sophie isn't at the park and she isn't at school. Alex isn't with Matt and he isn't at the park. Matt isn't at the beach. Jenny isn't with Alex and she isn't with Matt.

1 *Sophie* is at the beach.

2 _____ is at the park.

3 _____ is at the beach.

4 _____ is at school.

Adjectives

1 Circle the adjectives. Match them with the pictures.

sad bored x g h o t r h happy u l y thirsty ri cold m n k tired r h s a d hungry o u

to be: questions

3 ☆ Complete Mr Big's questions. Use *are, is* or *am*.

1 **_Am_** I at home?
2 _____ you at school now?
3 _____ Billy an octopus?
4 _____ Oscar and Jo-Jo brother and sister?
5 _____ we at the park?

4 ☆ Look at the questions in Exercise 3. Tick the true answers.

1 a ☐ Yes, you are.   b ✓ No, you aren't.
2 a ☐ Yes, I am.   b ☐ No, I'm not.
3 a ☐ Yes, he is.   b ☐ No, he isn't.
4 a ☐ Yes, they are. b ☐ No, they aren't.
5 a ☐ Yes, you are.   b ☐ No, you aren't.

5 ☆☆ Write Mr Big's questions. Then write true answers.

1 Jo-Jo / sad?
  Is Jo-Jo sad?   _No, she isn't._
2 you / tired?
  _____
  _____
3 I / a dog?
  _____
  _____
4 the magic mirror / here?
  _____
  _____
5 Jo-Jo and Oscar / at home?
  _____
  _____

2 Complete the sentences. Make them true for you.

1 At school I am _____ .
2 With my friends I am _____ .
3 At the park I am _____ .
4 At the beach I am _____ .

6 ☆☆☆ Write questions for these answers.

1 _Are they at the park?_
No, they aren't. They're at home.

2 _____
No, I'm not. I'm happy.

3 _____
Yes, we are. We're with the teacher.

4 _____
No, she isn't. She's at work.

5 _____
No, they aren't. They're thirsty.

6 _____
Yes, he is. Oscar's ten and Jo-Jo's eleven.

Asking how you feel

7 Order the sentences.

Shark   are   How   you   today ?
1 _How are you today?_
Billy   thank   Fine,   you   .
2 _____
   are   How   you   ?
3 _____
Shark   great   Not .
4 _____
   hungry   I'm   !
5 _____

8 Complete this dialogue between you and your friend.

You   Hi, ¹_____ (name).
           How ²_____ _____ today?
Your friend ³_____ _____ fine, _____ .
           How ⁴_____ you?
You   ⁵_____ _____ .

9 Complete the letters. Use these words. Add the sticker of Jo-Jo's photo.

are   H̶i̶   you   How   I'm   granny   cool

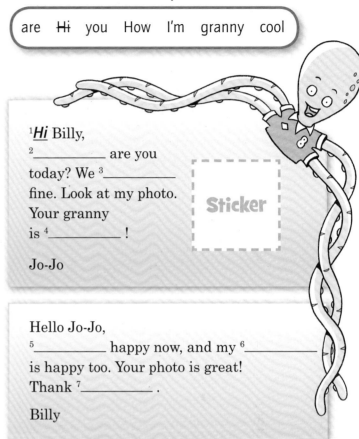

¹_Hi_ Billy,
²_____ are you today? We ³_____ fine. Look at my photo. Your granny is ⁴_____ !

Jo-Jo

Sticker

Hello Jo-Jo,
⁵_____ happy now, and my ⁶_____ is happy too. Your photo is great! Thank ⁷_____ .

Billy

Mr Big's Learning Blog

Remember new words

Draw pictures to remember new words.

happy   thirsty

Skills

Reading

1 Read the email. Tick (✓) the picture of Harry's cake.

Ⓐ ☐ Ⓑ ☐

Hi Granny,

The red bag from you and Granddad is fantastic. The octopus card is cool too. Thank you!

Are you at home today? Are you hungry? We're at home and my birthday cake is here. It's a big, blue shark. It's great!

Love from

Harry

2 Read the email again. True or false?

1 The bag is from Granny and Granddad. *true*
2 The bag is red. _____
3 The birthday cake is at school. _____
4 The cake is green. _____
5 The cake isn't nice. _____

Happy Birthday!

smile!

Writing

3 It's your birthday. Write a 'thank you' email.

Hi _____ ,

The _____ from you and

_____ is _____ !

The _____ is

_____ too.

_____ _____ !

Love _____

_____

② Countries

My Picture Dictionary

Countries

1 Complete the words.

1 A_r_ _g_ _e_ _n_ _t_ _i_ _n_ _a_   2 P_ _ _ _ _d   3 C_ _ _ a   4 B_ _ _ _ _ _n

5 T_ _ _ _ _y   6 E_ _ _ _t   7 A_ _ _ _ _ _ _ _a   8 G_ _ _ _ _e

9 P_ _ _ _ _ _l   10 t_ _ _ _A   11 R_ _ _ _ _a   12 B_ _ _ _l

my words

Find more countries. Write them here.

_____

_____

Discover **5** extra words. Go to page 71.

Pen Pals

Places

1 Match the words with the places.

mountain   lake   river **1**   sea   island   village   town   city

Sticker

2 Write words from Exercise 1 in the puzzle.

```
        ¹C  I  T  Y
   ²       V
        ³
     ⁴          G  E
  ⁵M
        ⁶T
  ⁷     L
```

3 Complete the sentence with the magic word and add the sticker.

The places in Exercise 1 are in **I**_____ .

a / an

4 ☆ Circle the correct word.

1 My home is in Killarney, (a) / an town in Ireland.
2 Killarney is on a / an lake.
3 Ireland is a / an island.
4 It isn't a / an hot country.
5 Today I'm at a / an fantastic beach.
6 My things are in a / an orange bag.
7 A / An octopus is in the sea.

who? / where?

5 ☆ Complete the questions. Use *who* or *where*.

1 A *Where* is your mum?
B She's at work.
2 A _____ are we?
B We're in the mountains.
3 A _____ is she?
B She's my sister, Karolina.
4 A _____ is the ball?
B It's in the sea.
5 A _____ are Ola and João?
B They're my penpals.
6 A _____ is Mr Grant?
B He's my teacher.
7 A _____ are you from?
B I'm from Krakow in Poland.

6 ☆☆ Order the questions. Match them with the answers.

1 | are | Alex and Sophie | who | ?
Who are Alex and Sophie?

2 | are | where | Moscow and St Petersburg | ?
_____

3 | who | Elizabeth II | is | ?
_____

4 | from | are | where | Scarlett Johansson
| and Johnny Depp | ?
_____
_____

5 | where | the River Yangtze | is | ?
_____

a They're in Russia.
b It's in China.
c They're kids in this book. *1*
d They're from the USA.
e She's the queen of Britain.

7 ☆☆☆ Write the questions and answer them.

1 who / your teacher?
Who is your teacher?
My teacher is … _____
2 who / your friends?
_____
_____
3 where / you / from?
_____
_____
4 where / you / now?
_____
_____

Capital letters

8 Complete the words with these letters. Use a capital letter when necessary.

| h | t | s | j | b | g | s | m̶ | a | f | a |

¹*M*att is ² *f* rom ³__ ritain. Today ⁴__ e is at
⁵__ chool with ⁶__ lex, ⁷__ ophie and ⁸__ enny.
The ⁹__ eacher, Mr Williams, is from ¹⁰__ ustralia.
He's ¹¹__ reat.

9 Do the quiz. Match the columns.

1 **Lake Baikal**   a is a sea.
2 The Amazon   b are mountains.
3 **The Mediterranean**   c is a lake in Russia.
4 The Himalayas   d is a river in Brazil.
5 Crete   e is a city in Britain.
6 London   f is an island.

2ᵇ Cool Jobs

Jobs

1 Circle the jobs.

*dancter*b*singer*uf*football player*lco*sactress*i*w
*M*i*ss*du*actors*i*dan*cerkbasing

3 Write names to make true sentences.

1 *Will Smith* is a famous actor.
2 _____ is a great football player.
3 _____ is a fantastic singer.
4 _____ is a good actress.
5 _____ is a cool dancer.

2 Label the pictures with the words from Exercise 1.

1 *actor*   2 _____   3 _____

4 _____   5 _____

Possessive adjectives

4 ☆ Complete. Use a possessive adjective. Keep the same meaning.

1 a You are Alex and Sophie.   b *Your* names are Alex and Sophie.
2 a I'm Jenny.   b _____ name is Jenny.
3 a You are Matt.   b _____ name is Matt.
4 a She is Maria Sharapova.   b _____ name is Maria Sharapova.
5 a They are Vanessa and Ed.   b _____ names are Vanessa and Ed.
6 a He is Cristiano Ronaldo.   b _____ name is Cristiano Ronaldo.
7 a We are Will and Jaden Smith.   b _____ names are Will and Jaden Smith.
8 a It is Chicago.   b _____ name is Chicago.

5 ☆☆ Complete the dialogue. Use these words.

you   We   ~~your~~   Its   his   I   It
My   Our   he

Ethan	Hi. I'm Ethan. What's ¹*your* name?
Marilyn	² _____ name is Marilyn Moody.
Ethan	What's your job?
Marilyn	³ _____ 'm a famous dancer. My brother Troy is a singer.
Ethan	Is ⁴ _____ famous too?
Marilyn	Yes, ⁵ _____ songs are very famous.
Ethan	Where are ⁶ _____ from?
Marilyn	We're from Britain. ⁷ _____ home is in a town in Australia now. ⁸ _____ name is Elliston.
Ethan	Is it a nice town?
Marilyn	⁹ _____ 's great. ¹⁰ _____ 're very happy here.

Reading

6 Look at the factfile. Complete the dialogue.

Name:
Miley Cyrus

Job:
actress and singer

Country:
the USA

Dad:
Billy Ray Cyrus

A   Who is this?
B   Her name is ¹*Miley Cyrus* .
A   What's her ² _____ ?
B   She's an actress and a ³ _____ .
A   Is she famous?
B   Yes, she is. She's in *Hannah Montana*. Her dad is in *Hannah Montana* too. His name is
⁴ _____ .
A   Where are they from?
B   They're from Nashville. It's a city in
⁵ _____ .

Talking Tips!

7 Complete the dialogues. Use these words.

I'm sorry   ~~Here you are~~   Smile
Watch out   Cool

1 A   Oh no! Where's my pen?
   B   *Here you are.*
2 A   Am I in the photo?
   B   Yes, you are. _____ !
3 A   My dad's a football player.
   B   _____ !
4 A   Look! A shark!
   B   Oh no! _____ !
5 A   Your school work isn't here. Where is it, Max?
   B   It's at home, Mr Jones. _____ .

Puzzle Zone

8 Complete the jobs.
1 My brother is an a c t o r.
2 My granny is an __ __ __ __ __ s s.
3 My granddad is a __ __ n g __ __ .
4 My mum is a __ a n __ __ .
5 My dad is a f __ __ __ b __ __ __ p __ __ __ __ __ …

9 Write the magic letters and add the sticker.
… and I'm a __ __ __h__ __ __ .

Sticker

19

Regular plural nouns

1 ☆ Write the plurals.

1 baby   *babies*
2 bus   _____
3 school   _____
4 beach   _____
5 family   _____
6 lake   _____
7 actor   _____
8 box   _____
9 spy   _____
10 brother   _____

2 ☆☆ Count and write.

pyramid ~~pen~~ box granny

1 *seven pens*   2 _____
3 _____   4 _____

3 ☆☆☆ Write the plural sentences.

1 The pyramid isn't in Greece.
The pyramids aren't in Greece.
2 The dancer is fantastic.
_____
3 The city isn't big.
_____
4 The teacher is from Britain.
_____
5 The bus isn't red.
_____

Mr Big's Learning Blog

Use English!

Always use English when you ask your teacher for translations.

Asking for translations

4 Complete the questions and answers.

1 *What's* [bus] *in* *English* ?

It's *bus* .

2 _____ [pencil] ____ ____ ?

It's _____ .

3 _____ [mountain] ____ ____ ?

It's _____ .

4 _____ [dog] ____ ____ ?

It's _____ .

5 _____ [fields] ____ ____ ?

It's _____ .

6 _____ [football player] ____ ____ ?

It's _____ .

Reading

5 Read the text and complete labels 1–4. Add the sticker.

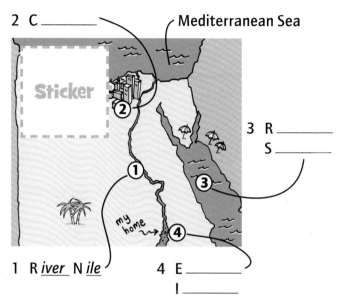

2 C_____   Mediterranean Sea

3 R _____
  S _____

1 R *iver* N *ile*   4 E _____
             I _____

Hi. My name's Mahmoud. I'm eleven and I'm from Egypt. My home is in a village on Elephantine Island. The island isn't in a lake or a sea – it's in the River Nile. The pyramids in Egypt are very famous. They're at Giza. Cairo is a big city on the Nile. The beaches on the Red Sea are famous too. My country is great!

★ Puzzle Zone ★

6 Look at the book. Write the questions and answers.

In Egypt

Yes   نعم
No   لا

In China

Hello   你好
Goodbye   再見

In Greece

How are you?   Τι κάνετε
Fine, thank you.   Καλά, ευχαριστώ

In Russia

Please   Пожалуйста
Thank you   Спасибо

1   *What's* 你好 *in* *English* ?
It's *Hello* .

2   _____ Τι κάνετε
_____ ?
It's _____ .

3   _____ لا _____
_____ ? It's _____

4   _____ Спасибо
_____ ?
It's _____ .

2ᵈ Let's Revise!

Vocabulary

1 Vocabulary race! Write as many words as you can in one minute.

Places	Jobs	Feelings	Family	Colours
lake				
home				

(½ point per word)   __/10

2 Write countries in the puzzle. Complete the sentence with the magic word.

```
1
C  H  I  N  A
         2
         T  _  _  _  Y
      3
         U  _  _
4
E  G  _
            5
            G  _  _  C
         6
         B  _  _  I
            7
            P  _  _  N  D
8
A  _  G  _  T
9
P  _  _  T  _  L
```

Elizabeth II is queen in Britain and _____ .

__/8

Grammar

3 Circle the correct word.

1 James Bond is ⓐ / an spy from Britain.
2 **You** / **Your** birthday cake is nice.
3 Brazil is **a** / **an** hot country.
4 What are **they** / **their** names?
5 My mum is **at** / **at the** work today.
6 **He** / **His** is from China.
7 **Where** / **Who** is the River Nile?
8 This is **a** / **an** apple.
9 **Where** / **Who** is from a village?
10 Are your friends **at** / **at the** park?

__/9

4 Complete. Use the correct form of the word in brackets.

1 What **is** (be) your name?
2 Look – two red _____ (bus)!
3 The _____ (beach) in Egypt are great.
4 My brothers _____ (be) bored.
5 I _____ (not be) from a big city.
6 _____ (be) you and your dad thirsty?
7 No, we _____ (not be).
8 The four _____ (country) in Britain are England, Scotland, Wales and Northern Ireland.
9 Your _____ (sister) are nice.

__/8

Functions

5 Match the questions with the answers.

1 What's your name?   a I'm twelve.
2 What's *Hola* in English?   b My name's Lucy.
3 How are you today?   c It's *Hello*.
4 How do you spell *Hello*?   d H-E-L-L-O.
5 How old are you?   e 623971.
6 What's your phone number?   f Not great.

__/5

Your score	Your total score
	__/40

😃 30–40   🙂 20–30   ☹ 0–20

22

3 Favourites

My Picture Dictionary

Favourite things

1 Complete the words.

1 s _k a t e_ b _o a r_ d
2 c __ m p __ __ __ __ __
   g __ __ __
3 r __ b __ __
4 c __ __
5 C __ pl __ y __ __
6 pl __ __ __
7 w __ __ c h
8 k __ t __
9 c __ m __ __ a

2 Label the pictures with the words from Exercise 1.

① _____

② _____

③ _____

④ _____

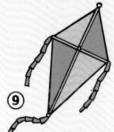
⑤ _____

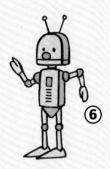
⑥ _____

⑦ _____

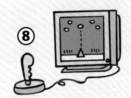
⑧ _____

⑨ _____

3 Write words from Exercise 1 in the puzzle. Answer the question with the magic word.

```
              ¹C D P L A Y E R
             ²R
                  ³K
⁴C
                  ⁵C
        ⁶S
             ⁷P
```

What's the favourite computer game in the world? _____

Discover **5** extra words. Go to page 71.

my words

What are your favourite things? Write them here.

_____
_____
_____
_____
_____
_____

3ᵃ At The Shop

this, that

1 ⭐ Look at the picture. Write a–f.

1 this car — [a]
2 that plane — [ ]
3 this watch — [ ]
4 this plane — [ ]
5 that car — [ ]
6 that watch — [ ]

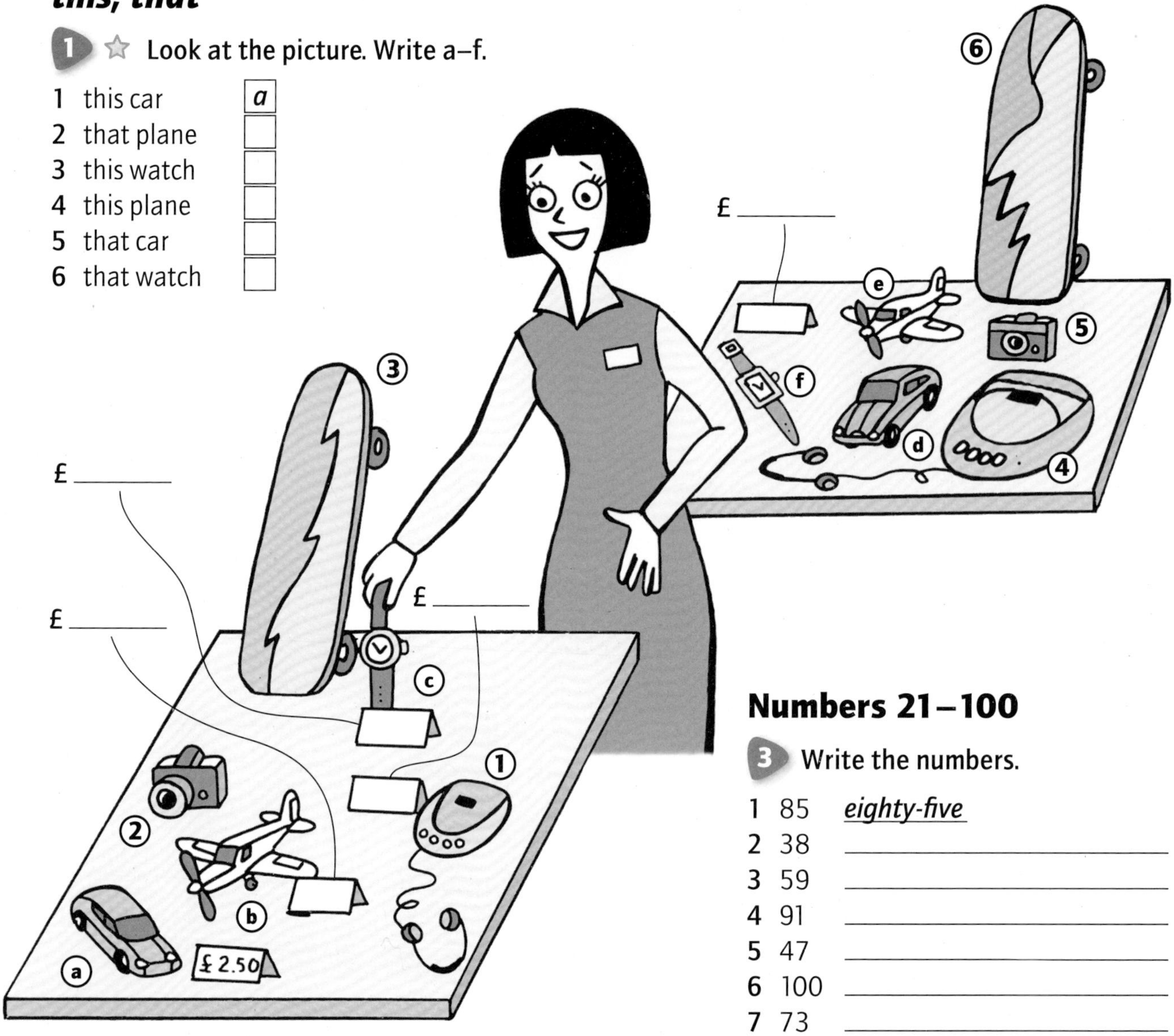

£ _____
£ _____
£ _____
£ _____
£ 2.50

Numbers 21–100

3 Write the numbers.

1 85 *eighty-five*
2 38 _____
3 59 _____
4 91 _____
5 47 _____
6 100 _____
7 73 _____
8 62 _____

2 ⭐⭐ Find 1–6 in the picture and write sentences.

1 (great) *This CD player is great.*
2 (orange) _____
3 (cool) _____
4 (big) _____
5 (green) _____
6 (fantastic) _____

4 Find the things in the picture. Write the prices.

1 'This car is two pounds fifty.'
2 'This CD player is sixty pounds.'
3 'That watch is eleven pounds ninety-nine.'
4 'This plane is one pound eighty.'
5 'This watch is six pounds seventy-five.'

Shopping

5 Look at the word spiral and write the dialogue.

A *Excuse me, how* _____ ?
B _____ .
A _____ ? _____ !
B _____ .
A _____ .

6 Complete the dialogue. What does Alex buy? Add the sticker.

Sticker

Alex	E*xcuse* m*e* , h_____ m*uch* i_____ that green thing?
Woman	This green kite?
Alex	No, that green thing in the yellow shirt.
Woman	It's one pound thirty-nine.
Alex	O*ne* p_____ t_____ ? O*kay* !
Woman	H*ere* y_____ a_____ .
Alex	T_____ y*ou* .

Puzzle Zone

7 Add (+) the numbers in the pyramid.

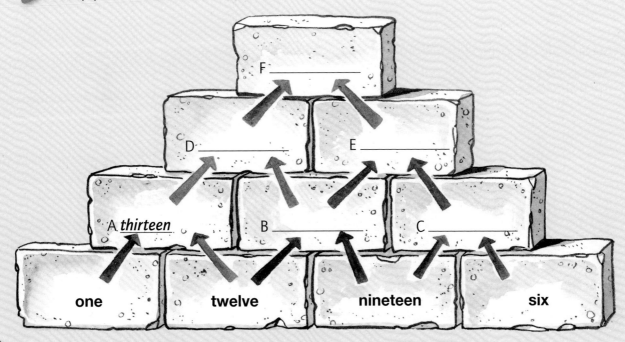

F _____

D _____   E _____

A *thirteen*   B _____   C _____

one   twelve   nineteen   six

Adjectives

1 Match the opposites.

1	big	a	slow
2	short	b	old
3	ugly	c	small
4	new	d	long
5	fast	e	beautiful

2 Look at the picture and complete the text with words from Exercise 1.

Car A is ¹n <u>e w</u>. It's very ²l _ _ _ and very ³f _ _ _.
Car B is ⁴b _ _ _ _ _ _ _ _ _.
Car C is ⁵s _ _ _ _ and ⁶u _ _ _.
Car D is ⁷o _ _. It's ⁸b _ _ and ⁹s _ _ _.

3 Circle the adjectives and colours. Write them in the puzzle.

The things in my collection are small and white. They are beautiful, but one is long and ugly. They are from the beach. What are they?

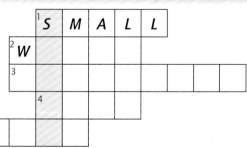

```
1 S M A L L
2 W
3
  4
5
```

4 Complete the answer with the magic word. Add the sticker.

They're _____.

Sticker

5 Write true sentences about your things. Use different adjectives.

1 *My pencils are long.*
2 _____
3 _____
4 _____
5 _____
6 _____

⭐ **Puzzle Zone** ⭐

6 Cross out one letter in each square. Write four adjectives.

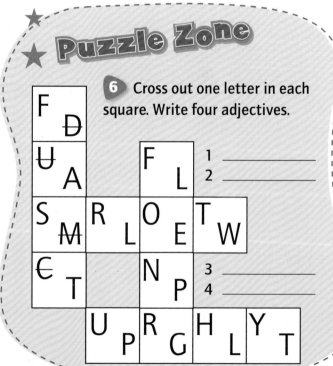

1 _____
2 _____
3 _____
4 _____

Possessive 's

7 ☆ **Circle the correct word.**

1 My **friend** / **friend's** bike is yellow.
2 That **kite** / **kite's** is from Russia.
3 My **dad** / **dad's** camera is fantastic.
4 **Charlie** / **Charlie's** favourite thing is his skateboard.
5 My **granny** / **granny's** is fifty-three.
6 Is your **brother** / **brother's** at school today?

8 ☆ **Look at the table and complete the sentences.**

	Matt	Jenny	Alex	Sophie
Favourite thing	my robot	my dog	my guitar	my computer game
Favourite colour	red	blue	green	pink
Favourite place	the park	the beach	the mountains	my home

1 _Matt's_ favourite thing is his robot.
2 _____ favourite colour is blue.
3 _____ favourite place is her home.
4 _____ favourite thing is his guitar.
5 _____ favourite place is the beach.
6 _____ favourite colour is green.

9 ☆☆ **Look at the table again. Write questions for these answers.**

1 _What's Jenny's favourite thing?_
  Her dog.
2 _____
  The park.
3 _____
  Pink.
4 _____
  Her computer game.
5 _____
  The mountains.
6 _____
  Red.

10 ☆☆☆ **Write about you and your friends or family.**

1 My favourite _colour_ is _black_ .
2 My favourite _____ is _____ .
3 My favourite _____ is _____ .
4 _____'s favourite _____ is _____ .
5 _____'s favourite _____ is _____ .
6 _____'s favourite _____ is _____ .

these, those

 1 ☆ Write the plural.

1 this mirror **these** mirrors
2 that game _____ games
3 that boy _____ boys
4 this girl _____ girls
5 that country _____ countries
6 this bus _____ buses

 2 ☆ Complete. Use *this*, *that*, *these* or *those*.

1 Look at **that** dragon!

2 _____ dragon is a baby.

3 _____ dragons are its mum and dad.

4 _____ dragon isn't nice.

5 _____ dragons are our friends!

 3 ☆☆☆ Write the plural sentences.

1 That car is fast.
Those cars are fast.
2 This skateboard is new.
_____
3 This kite is very long.
_____
4 That watch is old.
_____
5 That spy is cool.
_____
6 This actress is very famous.
_____

Irregular plural nouns

4 ☆ Complete the table.

	Singular	Plural
1	*man*	men
2	woman	_____
3	child	_____
4	_____	people

5 ☆☆ Complete the sentences. Use words from Exercise 4.

1 Jo-Jo's favourite **person** is her granddad.
2 Jo-Jo is eleven and Oscar is ten. They are
   _____ .
3 Mr Big's favourite _____ are Jo-Jo, Oscar
   and their mum and dad.
4 Dads and granddads are _____ , but mums
   aren't.
5 Mums and grannies are _____ , but dads
   aren't.
6 I am a _____ , but my teacher isn't.
7 My teacher, Mr Brown, is a _____ .

Talking Tips!

6 Complete the dialogue. Use these words.

> Hurry up ~~Watch out~~ Here you are
> Are you OK

Oscar   Look at that dog with Mr Big.

Jo-Jo   Oh no! That dog isn't nice. [1]*Watch out*, Mr Big!

Oscar   [2]_____, Jo-Jo! Come and help Mr Big!

Jo-Jo   Mr Big! Mr Big! [3]_____?

Mr Big   Woof! Woof!

Oscar   Yes, he is. He's fine.

Jo-Jo   Look, Mr Big, this is your favourite thing. [4]_____.

Puzzle Zone

7 Start with B. Miss a letter, then write a letter. Add the sticker in the heart.

S O J U O R J I O T B E I P T E L R Y S S O F N A I V

Sticker

B I L _ _ _ _ _ _ _ _ _ _ _ _ _
_ _ _ _ _ _ _ _ _ _ _ _ _ _

8 Complete the letters. Use these words.

> this   fast   brother's   game   these
> ~~people~~   women

Hi Billy,

We're the [1]*people* in a computer [2]_____ today but [3]_____ game isn't nice! The men and [4]_____ here aren't our friends, and [5]_____ dragons are big and [6]_____ .
Help!

Love from

Jo-Jo

Hi Jo-Jo,

Come here soon and play my [7]_____ computer games. They're great!

Love from

Billy

Mr Big's Learning Blog

Remember irregular plurals

Keep a page in your vocabulary notebook for words with irregular plurals.

Reading

1 Look and read. What is the class's favourite game?

_____

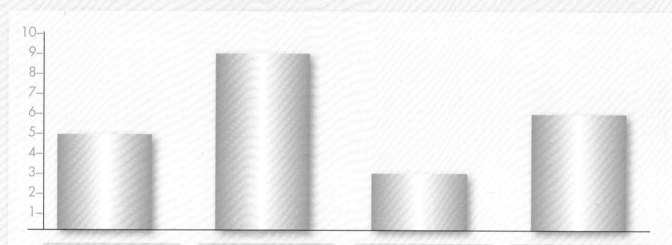

My favourite game is *Go! Dogs*. The black and white dogs are beautiful.

Emily, 10

Fun Sports is great. Tennis is my favourite sport in the game.

Callum, 11

Robot Run! is a very good game. Dimi is a small robot and Rolo is an old robot. They're cool.

Nita, 9

We're good *Purple Dragons* players. It's our favourite game.

Ben and William, 12

2 True or false? Correct the false sentences.

1 *Fun Sports* is ten people's favourite game.
   false It is nine people's favourite game.

2 *Robot Run!* is three people's favourite game.

   _____

3 Emily's favourite game is *Fun Sports*.

   _____

4 Dimi and Rolo are dogs.

   _____

5 Ben and William are bad *Purple Dragons* players.

   _____

Writing

3 Complete the paragraph about computer games or other games.

My favourite game is

_____ .

It's _____ .

My friend's favourite game is

_____ .

It's _____ .

Pets

My Picture Dictionary

Pets

1 Look at the pets. Write pets 1–8 and find the answers.

What are Australia's favourite pets?

¹B	I		
	²H		
³D			
	⁴S		

What is Australia's favourite pet name?

	O	
⁵F		
	⁶C	
⁷R		
⁸H		

2 Match the words with the animals.

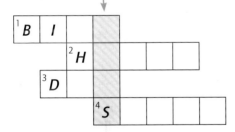

1 big or small   a snake
2 very big   b dog
3 very long   c hamster
4 big or small, long or short   d rabbit
5 very small   e fish
6 small   f horse

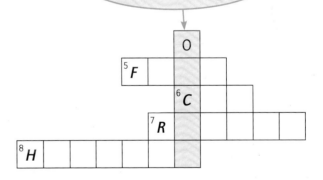

my words

What are your favourite pets?
Write them here.

_____
_____
_____
_____

Discover 5 extra words. Go to page 71.

4a A Lost Pet

Body parts

1 Complete the words.

1 a **r** m
2 b _ _ y
3 n _ s _
4 t o _ _ h
5 l _ g
6 _ y e
7 f _ o _
8 e _ r
9 m _ u _ h
10 h _ a _
11 t _ _ l

2 Count the body parts and write the plural of the words from Exercise 1.

1 two **arms**
2 three _____
3 four _____ , _____ , _____ ,
_____
4 eight _____
5 fourteen _____ , _____

have got / has got: affirmative

3 ☆ Complete. Use *have got* or *has got*.

Freya

Hi, I'm Freya.
I [1] **have got** a job at the Lost Pets Home.
We [2] _____ two dogs here today. Their names are Bess and Tess.
They [3] _____ short legs, and Tess [4] _____ spots.
We [5] _____ a cat. His name is Max. He [6] _____ big eyes. The home [7] _____ rabbits, hamsters and birds too. I [8] _____ a fantastic job!

4 ☆ Look at the picture in Exercise 2 and complete the sentences.

1 *Bess and Tess have got* short legs.
2 _____ big teeth.
3 _____ long ears.
4 _____ long bodies.
5 _____ long legs.
6 _____ a long tail.

5 ☆☆ Look in the mirror and write about you.

I've got… _____

_____

_____

_____

_____

_____

_____

_____

6 ⭐⭐ Read the texts and complete the information about the lost pets.

① *Rambo is one and he is a hamster. He has got a brown body. He has got white legs and white feet.*

LOST PETS HOME
Name: Rambo
Animal: _hamster_
How old? _1_
Colour:
brown body, white legs and feet

② *Munch and Crunch are rabbits. They have got white bodies, black spots and pink eyes. They are two.*

LOST PETS HOME
Name: Munch and Crunch
Animal: _____
How old? _____
Colour:
_____

③ *Arthur has got a blue and green body and a red and yellow head. He is fifty. He is a bird.*

LOST PETS HOME
Name: Arthur
Animal: _____
How old? _____
What colour:
_____

7 ⭐⭐⭐ Find the sticker for one of the pets.

This is
_____

Sticker

8 ⭐⭐⭐ Find six differences. Write sentences.

Maisy   Daisy

Puzzle Zone

9 ⭐⭐ Match and make eight body parts.

ar **dy** gs   **rs** se

ET   ms   **le**   **bo** NO

              ey   **fe**

he **ea**   **es**   ad

1 _arms_   5 _____
2 _____   6 _____
3 _____   7 _____
4 _____   8 _____

1 Maisy has got one white ear and one black ear. Daisy has got two white ears.

2 _____
3 _____
4 _____
5 _____
6 _____

4b A Phone Call

have got, has got: negative

1 ☆ **Look at the picture. Write the person or pet.**

1 This pet hasn't got a long tail.
   the rabbit
2 These people haven't got long noses.
   _____ and _____
3 These children haven't got skateboards.
   _____ and _____
4 This pet hasn't got spots.
   _____
5 This person hasn't got a pet.
   _____

2 ☆ **Complete Brandon's sentences.**
Use *haven't got* or *hasn't got*. Look at the picture.
Tick Brandon's true sentences.

1 I *haven't got* a brother. ✓
2 We _____ a big car.
3 My sister's dog _____ short legs.
4 My mum _____ a hamster.
5 My mum and dad _____ skateboards.
6 My rabbit _____ long ears.
7 My big sister _____ a dog.
8 I _____ a big mouth.

3 ☆☆ **Write the contractions.**

1 That bird <u>has got</u> a blue head.
   That bird's got a blue head.
2 It <u>has not got</u> arms.
   _____
3 I <u>have not got</u> a tail.
   _____
4 I <u>have got</u> a fantastic granddad.
   _____
5 He <u>has got</u> big ears.
   _____

4 ☆☆ **Pet quiz! Write *have got*, *has got*, *haven't got* or *hasn't got*. Then look at the bottom of page 35 and correct your work.**

1 A cat *hasn't got* arms.
2 Dogs _____ forty-two teeth.
3 A fish _____ ears.
4 A bird _____ a nose.
5 Hamsters _____ tails.
6 Snakes _____ ears.

34

5 ☆☆ Find two mistakes in each description 1–4.
Add a sticker to text 5.

1 This dragon is from China. It's got twenty legs, small teeth and a long tail.
It hasn't got small teeth and it hasn't got twenty legs.

2 Ra is from Egypt. He's got a bird's head, a dog's body and a snake's tail.
_____
_____

Sticker

3 Centaurs are from Greece. They've got a cat's body, a hamster's head and a horse's legs.
_____
_____

4 Cerberus is from Greece. He's a very big dog. He's got three heads, six legs and three tails.
_____
_____

5 Ngariman is from Australia. He's got a man's body, a cat's head and a cat's tail.

Making a phone call

6 Order the lines in the dialogue.

LOST: DRAGON ROBOT
Please phone Jamie: 274620

☐ Jamie Fantastic!

☐ Amber Hi. Is that Jamie?

1 Jamie Hello?

☐ Amber Oh, hello. My name's Amber. I've got a dragon robot here. Maybe it's your lost dragon robot.

☐ Jamie Yes, that's my dragon robot. Thanks!

☐ Amber It's red and green and it's got a very big mouth.

☐ Jamie Yes, it is.

7 Complete the dialogue. Use these words.

Is   Thanks   is   it   ~~Hello~~   that

Sveta   ¹*Hello*?
Cristiano Hi. ² _____ ³ _____ Sveta?
Sveta   Yes, ⁴ _____ ⁵ _____ .
Cristiano Oh, hello. I'm at the park, and your school bag is here! It's got your name and phone number on it.
Sveta   ⁶ _____ !

cat/arms ✗   dogs/forty-two teeth ✓   fish/ears ✗
bird/nose ✓   hamster/tail ✓   snakes/ears ✗

The Magic Mirror

Have got / has got: questions

1 ☆ **Complete the questions. Use *have*, *has* or *got*.**

1 ***Has*** Zingbat got pets in his shop?
2 _____ we got those pets in our world?
3 Have grobs _____ big mouths?
4 _____ the twink got five heads?
5 _____ Oscar and Jo-Jo got a pet dog?

2 ☆ **Match the answers with the questions in Exercise 1.**

a No, they haven't.   _____
b Yes, he has.   *1*
c Yes, they have.   _____
d No, it hasn't.   _____
e No, we haven't.   _____

3 ☆ **Write Oscar's questions.**

Zingbat's pet shop			
Pets	heads	ears	eyes
2 grobs	1	2 (short)	3
1 twink	1	2 (short)	2
4 daks	2	0	4
6 mubs	1	4	2
1 raz	1	2 (short)	2

1 Oscar ***Have you got*** (you) a twink?
   Yes, I have.
2 Oscar _____ (a twink) five eyes? No, it hasn't.
3 Oscar _____ (you) a pet with two heads? Yes, I have.
4 Oscar _____ (daks) eight eyes? No, they haven't.
5 Oscar _____ (a raz) long ears? Yes, it has.
6 Oscar _____ (mubs) four ears? Yes, they have.

4 ☆☆ **Look at Zingbat's chart in Exercise 3. Write questions for these answers.**

1 ***Have you got a mub?***
   Yes, I have.
2 _____
   No, I haven't.
3 _____
   No, they haven't.
4 _____
   Yes, it has.
5 _____
   Yes, I have.
6 _____
   No, it hasn't.
7 _____
   Yes, they have.

Talking Tips!

5 Complete the dialogue. Use these words.

> Here you are   I'm sorry   ~~Come on~~
> Really   Come and help

Mum   Homework, Sophie! ¹**_Come on_** !
Sophie But I haven't got a pen.
Mum   ² _____ ? Well, I've got a pen for you.
        ³ _____ .
Sophie Thank you. Hey, Mum. ⁴_____ !
        Please!
Mum   No, Sophie, not today. ⁵_____ , but
        I've got work too.

6 Complete the letters. Use these words.
Add the sticker of Billy's pet, Dip.

> ~~He's~~   hasn't   They've
> haven't   got   it

Dear Billy,

We're with Zingbat today. ¹**_He's_** got a
fantastic pet shop. It ²_____ got
dogs, but it's got a beautiful pet with
three legs. Have you ³_____ a
pet? Has ⁴_____ got arms and legs?

Love from

Jo-Jo

Dear Jo-Jo,

I've got two pets, Dip and Dap. ⁵_____
got five arms but they haven't got legs and
they ⁶_____ got a head!
Look at my picture of Dip!

Love from

Billy

> Sticker

Mr Big's Learning Blog

Remember numbers

Draw a pet shop. How many
animals are there?

_____

7 Read the text and find the English word for
the animal in the photo.

This animal is a _____ .

Noel Daniels has got seven pet tortoises.
Tortoises have got one head and four
feet … but the new baby hasn't! This
baby tortoise has got two heads. It's very
happy. The heads are good friends.
This is not the only animal in the world
with two heads. An animal collection in
the USA has got twenty-two snakes and
tortoises with two heads. Wow!

8 ☆☆☆ Read again and complete the
sentences with the numbers.

> 7   2   22   4   1

1 Tortoises have got _4_ feet.
2 Noel Daniels has got _____ tortoises.
3 He's got _____ tortoise with two heads.
4 The collection in the USA has got _____ animals.
5 The snakes in the collection have got _____ heads.

Let's Revise!

Vocabulary

1 Vocabulary race! Write as many words as you can in one minute.

Favourite things	Opposites	Pets	Body parts
kite	old		

(½ point per word) ___/12

2 Write the numbers in the boxes. Do the sums.

1 twenty [20] + seventeen [17] =*thirty-seven* [37]

2 twelve [ ] + forty [ ] = _____ [ ]

3 sixty [ ] + eleven [ ] = _____ [ ]

4 nine [ ] + ninety-one [ ] = _____ [ ]

5 sixty [ ] + twenty [ ] = _____ [ ]

___/4

Grammar

3 Complete the text with **'s** or the correct form of *have got*.

Oliver ¹*has got* two robots. They ²_____ big heads, but they ³_____ (not) big eyes.
His red robot is very old. It ⁴_____ (not) legs now and the robot ⁵_____ arms are lost too.
His green robot ⁶_____ head is very ugly, but it's his favourite. It ⁷_____ a skateboard.
⁸_____ you _____ a robot? ⁹_____ it ¹⁰_____ a skateboard?

___/8

4 Write 1–3 in the plural and 4–6 in the singular.

1 this foot   *these feet*
2 that child   _____
3 this woman   _____
4 those people _____
5 these men   _____
6 those teeth   _____

___/10

Functions

5 Order the sentences.

On the phone

Jenny   Hi. Game Zone   is   that
1 *Is that Game Zone* ?

Salesperson   is   it   yes
2 _____ , _____ .

Jenny   Where is your shop?

At the shop

Jenny   how much   Pet Island   is
3 _____ ?

Salesperson   pounds   fifteen
4 _____ .

Jenny   OK   pounds   fifteen
5 _____ ?
_____ !

Salesperson   you   here   are
6 _____ .

Jenny   thank   you
7 _____ .

___/6

Your score

Your total score
___/40

😃 30–40   🙂 20–30   🙁 0–20

5 Rooms

My Picture Dictionary

In the classroom

1 Complete the words for things in a classroom.

1 d _o_ _o_ r
2 l _ _ _ t
3 b _ _ _ _ c _ _ e
4 w _ _ d _ _

5 t _ b _ _ _
6 ch _ _ _ _
7 w _ _ l

8 d _ _ k
9 fl _ _ _
10 T _

2 Label the picture with the words in Exercise 1.

1 _____
2 _____
3 _____
4 _____
5 _____

6 _____
7 _____
8 _____
9 _____
10 _____

my words

What's in your classroom? Write the things here.

_____

_____

_____

Discover **5** extra words. Go to page 71.

39

in, on, under, next to

1 ☆ Look at the picture and write the names. Make a word with the first letter of each name and add the sticker.

What's under the TV?
A _s_ _ _ _ _ !

1 **_Sarah_** is under the table.
2 _____ is on the chair.
3 _____ is next to Noah.
4 _____ is in the bookcase.
5 _____ is next to the bookcase.

2 ☆☆ Write sentences about the picture.

1 Abby / the light   **_Abby is next to the light._**
2 Emma / the box   _____
3 Emma / the picture   _____
4 the box / the floor   _____
5 the chair / the window _____

3 ☆☆☆ Write three more sentences about the picture.

1 _____
_____
2 _____
_____
3 _____
_____

Talking about where things are

4 Write the questions. Match the questions with the answers.

1 [are] [Where] [books] [the]
**Where are the books?**
2 [Where] [our] [is] [teacher] ?
_____
3 [my] [are] [computer games] [Where] ?
_____
4 [your] [is] [Where] [homework] ?
_____

a It's in my bag.
b They're under your desk.
c They're in the bookcase. _**1**_
d He's in the classroom.

5 Answer the questions.

1 Where's your bag?
It's… _____

2 Where's your English book?
_____

3 Where are your pens and pencils?
_____

4 Where is your desk?
_____

Talking Tips!

6 Complete the dialogues. Use these words.

Really	~~Here you are~~	Good luck
We're late	Cool	

A I've got your lucky hat. ¹**Here you are.**
B ²_____ ! Thanks.
A ³_____ in your tennis game.

C That's the plane to London.
D ⁴_____ ?
E Yes. Hurry up! ⁵_____ .

★ Puzzle Zone ★

7 Where is Matt's lucky hat? Cross out the other hats and complete the sentence.

It isn't under a chair.

It isn't on the door.

It isn't in the bag.

It isn't in the desk.

It isn't under the bookcase.

It isn't next to the light.

It isn't under the table.

It isn't next to the TV.

It isn't on the wall.

It isn't under the window.

Matt's lucky hat is
_____

Crazy Room Competition

there is / there are

1 ☆ Complete Jack's sentences about his bedroom. Use *There is* or *There are*.

1 *There are* books in my bookcase.
2 _____ one magazine on my desk.
3 _____ a light next to my bed.
4 _____ a ball under my desk.
5 _____ three robots in my box.
6 _____ a CD player on my bookcase.
7 _____ two shirts on my chair.

2 ☆☆ Look at the picture. Jack's bedroom is different today. Find and correct the false sentences in Exercise 1.

1 There are books under my chair.
_____
_____
_____

3 Why is Jack's room different today? Make a word from the letters on the bed and add the sticker.

His **p** __ __ __ __ __ is in his room.

4 ☆☆ Rewrite Mia's paragraph using contractions where possible.

> In my bedroom there is one red bed and there is one blue bed. There are tables next to the beds. There is a desk under the window and there is a light on the desk. There are two chairs.

In my bedroom there's one red bed and ...
_____
_____
_____

5 ☆☆☆ Write about your bedroom. Use some of these words.

> bed   chair   window   desk   light
> bookcase   TV   CD player

In my bedroom ...
_____
_____
_____

Sticker

Reading

6 Read and tick (✓).

Is your bedroom cool?

I In my bedroom there are:

❏ pink walls   ❏ purple walls

❏ black walls   ❏ green walls

❏ white walls   ❏ red walls

❏ blue walls   ❏ yellow walls

Are the walls your favourite colour(s)?

❏ yes   ❏ no

2 On the walls in my bedroom there are pictures of:

❏ my friends and family

❏ famous people

❏ pets

❏ beautiful places

Are your favourite people and things in the pictures?

❏ yes   ❏ no

3 What's cool for a bedroom?

❏ a beach design

❏ an under-the-sea design

❏ a football design

❏ a film design

Has your bedroom got your favourite design?

❏ yes   ❏ no

4 Is your bedroom your favourite place for homework?

❏ yes (my bed)

❏ yes (the floor in my bedroom)

❏ yes (the desk in my bedroom)

❏ no

4 YES answers: Cool bedroom!
2–3 YES answers: Your bedroom is nice, but it isn't fantastic.
0–1 YES answers: Oh no! You aren't happy in your bedroom. Ask your mum or dad for help.

Puzzle Zone

7 Complete the puzzle and find the magic word.

In the USA, what's the favourite colour for a girl's bedroom?

p _ _ _ _

①
②
③
④

	1					
	P	I	C	T	U	R	E

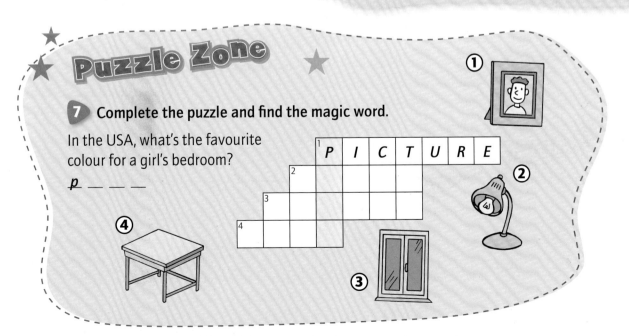

5c The Magic Mirror

Rooms

1 Circle the rooms and match with the pictures.

kitchentibathroomoshlivingroomebedroomulo

2 Look and complete the sentences.

1 My sister is in the _l i v i n g_ _r o o m_.

2 My dad is in the _ _ _ _ _ _ _ _ _ _ .

3 My granny is in the _ _ _ _ _ _ _ _ _ .

4 My mum is in the _ _ _ _ _ _ _ _ _ .

3 Write the magic letters and add the sticker.

Where am I?
I'm in the _l_ _ _ _ _ .

Sticker

4 Read and match with the pictures in Exercise 2. Then draw.

a There's a chair under the window in the bathroom. _2_

b There's a light next to the TV in the living room.

c There are three books on the table in the bedroom.

d There are two pictures on the wall in the kitchen.

5 Write sentences about rooms in your home. Use *there is* or *there are*.

1 *There are yellow walls in our living room.*
2 _____
3 _____
4 _____
5 _____

44

Is there … / Are there …?

6 ☆ Complete the dialogue. Use these words.

> there is   there are   there aren't   there isn't
> Is there (x2)   Are there (x2)

Oscar The TV in your living room is great.
¹**Are there** TVs with mouths in the bedrooms too?
Robot No, ²_____ .
Oscar ³_____ chairs with arms?
Robot Yes, ⁴_____ . I've got a chair with six arms in my bedroom.
Oscar ⁵_____ a bed with arms too?
Robot No, ⁶_____ , but there's a bed with a mouth. ⁷_____ a bed in your room?
Oscar Yes, ⁸_____ . It's got four legs, but it hasn't got a mouth.

7 ☆☆ Write questions with *Is there / Are there*. Look at the picture and write the answers.

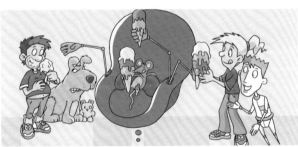

1 a dog / in the living room ?
Is there a dog in the living room?
Yes there is.
2 children / in the living room ?
_____
_____
3 a mouse / on the chair ?
_____
_____
4 tables / with arms ?
_____
_____
5 a TV / on the floor ?
_____
_____

8 Complete the letters. Use these words.

> are   ~~home~~   in   There's   under
> is   aren't   there

Hi Billy,

We're with a robot today. His ¹*home* is fantastic. ²_____ a TV with a mouth ³_____ the living room, and there ⁴_____ a chair with three arms! Are ⁵_____ chairs with three arms in your home ⁶_____ the sea?!

Love from

Jo-Jo

Hi Jo-Jo,

No, there ⁷_____ . Our chairs haven't got arms, but we're OK. There ⁸_____ five octopuses in my home, and forty arms!

Love from

Billy

Mr Big's Learning Blog

Use labels!

Put labels in English on things in your home. Say the word when you see the label.

chair

Skills

Reading

1 Read and choose.

This hotel is for:
a families with dogs
b people with lots of pets
c dogs

Dog's Dream Hotel

This fantastic hotel is next to the beach. There are forty beautiful bedrooms and a swimming pool, but the hotel isn't for people. It's for dogs.

The swimming pool

One of our bedrooms

There's a big bed in your dog's room. There are pictures of dogs and people on the walls, and the floors aren't cold. There's a good restaurant for the dogs at the hotel.

Dog's Dream Hotel   the place for happy dogs

2 Read the advert. True or false?

1 There's a beach next to the hotel. *true*
2 There are beds for the dogs. _____
3 The walls in the bedrooms have got pictures. _____
4 There are cold floors. _____
5 There's a restaurant for the families of the dogs. _____

Writing

3 Imagine a hotel for one of these. Write an advert.

cats horses robots sisters brothers

_____ **Hotel**

This fantastic hotel is for _____ .

There's a _____ and a _____ .

There are _____ .

There are _____ too.

_____

_____

Free Time

My Picture Dictionary

Activities

1 Complete the words.

1 p _l_ _a_ _y_ b _ _ _ _ _ _ _ _ _ _ _
2 p _ _ _ t _ _ _ _ _ _
3 s _ _ _
4 c _ _ _
5 d _ _ _ _
6 s _ _ _
7 r _ _ _ a b _ _ _
8 p _ _ _ the g _ _ _ _ _
9 d _ _ _
10 a _ _

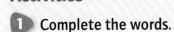

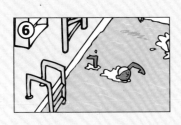

2 Write activities from Exercise 1 in the correct column for you.

At home	At school	At the park	In town

my words

What are your favourite activities? Write them here.

_____ _____ _____

_____ _____ _____

Discover **5** extra words. Go to page 71.

can / can't

1 ⭐ **Look at the pictures of Melvin and circle the right word.**

1 He **can** / **can't** play tennis.
2 He **can** / **can't** cook a fish.
3 He **can** / **can't** play the guitar.
4 He **can** / **can't** ride a horse.
5 He **can** / **can't** dance.

2 ⭐⭐ **Complete Melvin's sentences.**

1 I _**can sing**_ good songs.
2 I _____ basketball.
3 I _____ an apple.
4 I _____ football.
5 I _____ a bike.

3 ⭐⭐⭐ **Complete the sentences so they are true.**

1 _**My dad can't**_ ride a camel.
2 _____ sing songs in English.
3 _____ play computer games at home.
4 _____ make great cakes.
5 _____ swim from Britain to the USA.

⭐  ⭐

4 **Look at the maze and complete the poem with *can* or *can't*. Add the sticker.**

Sticker

My rabbit [1]_**can't**_ dance
But my snake [2]_____ swim.
My fish [3]_____ act
But my bird [4]_____ sing.
My dog [5]_____ dive
And my dog [6]_____ cook,
But he [7]_____ ride my bike.
Yes, it's true. Come and look!

Musical instruments

5 Complete the puzzle.

¹G			
²		³	
U			
I			⁴
T			
⁵			
A			
R			
	⁶			

6 Write sentences.

① Alex   ② Matt's brother   ③ Jenny

④ Jenny's granddad   ⑤ Sophie's sister   ⑥ Matt

1 *Alex can play the guitar.*

2 _____

_____

3 _____

_____

4 _____

_____

5 _____

_____

6 _____

_____

7 Read the text about Shakira. Write the missing words below.

Shakira is a famous singer. She can play

¹ and she can play ² too.

She can't play ³ and she can't play

⁴ , but she can play ⁵ . It's her

favourite sport.

1 *the guitar*   4 _____

2 _____   5 _____

3 _____

Days of the week

1 Find the days of the week.

S	A	T	U	R	D	A	Y	W
T	R	H	Y	E	M	F	C	E
F	G	U	X	J	O	B	P	D
R	O	R	S	I	N	E	A	N
I	M	S	U	N	D	A	Y	E
D	W	D	S	Q	A	J	I	S
A	H	A	G	D	Y	P	K	D
Y	F	Y	C	A	M	L	O	A
U	O	T	U	E	S	D	A	Y

2 Write the days in the correct order.

1 *Monday*
2 _____
3 _____
4 _____
5 _____
6 _____
7 _____

3 Look at Matt's diary and write sentences.

M	Granddad's birthday
T	
W	my basketball class
T	my English homework
F	
S	my basketball game
S	Sophie and Jenny's show

1 *Granddad's birthday is on Monday* .
2 _____ .
3 _____ .
4 _____ .
5 _____ .

Can you …?

4 ☆ Look at the table and write Jenny's answers.

	Me	Sophie	Matt	Alex
act	✗	✓	✗	✗
dance	✓	✓	✗	✓
sing	✗	✓	✓	✗
play the guitar	✗	✗	✗	✓
play basketball	✓	✗	✓	✓

1 Can you and Matt play the guitar?
   No, we can't.
2 Can Sophie dance?
   _____
3 Can Alex sing?
   _____
4 Can Matt and Alex play basketball?
   _____
5 Can you act?
   _____

5 ☆☆ Write questions for these answers.

1 Sophie/basketball *Can Sophie play basketball?*
   No, she can't.
2 Matt and Alex/act _____
   _____
   No, they can't.
3 you and Sophie/play the guitar _____
   _____
   No, we can't.
4 Sophie and Matt/sing _____
   _____
   Yes, they can.
5 you/dance _____
   _____
   Yes, I can.

Reading

6 Read the texts. Are the children right for the film? Tick (✓) or cross (✗).

Come and act in my new film.
Are you 8–12?
Can you act?
Can you ride a horse?
Yes? Phone Steven Steelberg now!
0107 459 3475

[✗] **Luke Simpson**
I can act and I can play the saxophone. I'm a good tennis player too. I'm ten.

[ ] **Cara O'Grady**
I can act and play the piano. I can ride a horse, but I can't swim. I'm nine.

[ ] **Sam Burns**
I'm a good actor and I can sing too. I'm eleven.

[ ] **Trisha and Trixie Truman**
We can sing and dance, and we can ride a horse. We're twelve.

Talking Tips!

7 Complete the dialogue. Use these words.

What a pity   It's a surprise   Here you are   ~~I'm sorry~~

Joe   Hi, Sasha. Can you come to the beach on Saturday? It's my birthday.
Sasha ¹ _I'm sorry_ , Joe. I can't.
Joe   ² _____!
Sasha But I've got this for you. ³ _____ !
Joe   Thanks. What is it?
Sasha ⁴ _____ . Happy birthday!

Puzzle Zone

8 Start with C. Miss a letter, then write a letter. Write the letters and answer the question. Add the sticker.

C̶ E A̶ A N̶
D   R
T   Sticker   Y
I   A
I R B U B O

C A N ___ ___ ___ ___
___ ___ ___ ___ ?

_____

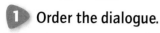

The Magic Mirror

6c

Making suggestions

1 Order the dialogue.

- [ ] A Yes, great! We can swim in the river too.
- [ ] B But we haven't got a ball. Let's play a computer game.
- [1] A I'm bored. Let's play football.
- [ ] B Well, let's go to the river. We can ride our bikes there.
- [ ] A Our games are at Oscar's house.

2 Write the suggestions.

1 This music is great. (dance)
   Let's dance

2 We haven't got homework today. (go to the park)
   _____ .

3 Look at that lake! (swim)
   _____ .

4 I've got a new computer game. (play)
   _____ .

5 We can't meet on Tuesday. (meet on Wednesday)
   _____ .

6 It's Mum's birthday. (make a cake)
   _____ .

7 We can't go in the car. (ride our bikes)
   _____ .

3 Complete the suggestions. Use *Let's* and these verbs.

go   ~~play~~   listen   play   meet

1 *Let's play* basketball.

2 _____ to the music.

3 _____ the man in the mirror.

4 _____ home.

5 _____ with the baby.

4 ☆☆☆ You and your friends are bored. Make suggestions with *Let's*.

| ~~go~~ swim sing play write cook dance |

1 *Let's go to Marek's house.*
2 _____
3 _____
4 _____
5 _____

5 Complete the letters. Use these words.

| I you swim ~~can't~~ play can aren't Let's |

Hi Billy,

I'm a good basketball player, but I ¹*can't* play with the people in the mirror. They ²_____ happy about my goal. Can ³_____ play basketball?

Love from

Jo-Jo

Hi Jo-Jo,

Yes, I ⁴_____ . I can ⁵_____ basketball with eight balls! I can ⁶_____ too, but ⁷_____ can't dive. ⁸_____ meet soon.

Love from

Billy

Mr Big's Learning Blog

Remember activity words

Record activity words in your vocabulary notebook in sentences.

I can *ride* a bike.

Let's *play* tennis.

Puzzle Zone

6 Go from the suggestions to the correct pictures (↑↗→↘↓↙←↖).

Minky the Mouse can play
_t_ _h_ _ _____ .

t Let's go to the beach.	l Let's play the piano.	o Let's act.
h Let's sing.	i Let's look at the fish.	i Let's dive.
v Let's ride a camel.	e Let's play tennis.	n 

7 Write the letters and complete the sentence. Add the sticker. Sticker

6d Let's Revise!

Vocabulary

1 Vocabulary race! Write as many words as you can in one minute.

In the classroom	Rooms	Activities	Musical instruments	Days of the week
door chair				

(½ point per word)   __/10

Grammar

2 Write true sentences. Use *can / can't*.

1 a fish / swim
  A fish can swim
2 a snake / ride a bike
  _____
3 football players / play / football
  _____
4 you / dive / in your living room
  _____
5 lots of singers / play / guitar
  _____

__/8

3 Write the questions and answers. Use *can* or *is / are there*.

1 you / sing / in the show? (✓)
  Can you sing in the show?
  Yes, I can.
2 James / play the piano? (✓)
  _____
  _____
3 a good piano / in the room? (✓)
  _____
  _____
4 good songs / in the show? (✗)
  _____
  _____
5 we / dance / on the piano? (✗)
  _____
  _____

__/8

4 Circle the correct words.

A ¹Can / (Let's) play tennis.
B OK. ²Where / There are the balls?
A Are they ³under / next the bed?
B No, they aren't, and they aren't ⁴in / on the floor.
A Well, let's ⁵play / can play basketball.
B Where ⁶is / to the basketball?
A It's here, ⁷next / on to the TV.
B Great! Let ⁸we / 's go.

__/14

Your score	Your total score
	__/40

😀 30–40   🙂 20–30   😟 0–20

54

Food

My Picture Dictionary

Food

1 Complete the words.

1 s_ _ _w_ch_ _
2 ch_ _ _e n
3 ch_ _ _l_ _ _ c_k_
4 r _i_ _c_ e
5 p_s_a

6 p_ _z_
7 ch_ _s
8 h_ _b_ _g_ _
9 f_s_
10 s_l_ _

2 Label the picture with the words from Exercise 1.

4 _rice_

3 Write the food in the picture in the correct column for you.

Discover **5** extra words. Go to page 71.

my words

What's your favourite food? Ask your teacher for new words.

_____   _____

_____   _____

_____   _____

It's Lunchtime!

Verbs

1 Write the verbs in the puzzle. Answer the question with the magic word.

What's the world's favourite food? _____

2 Write the words in the correct columns. Add two more things in each column.

> lunch   ~~in a house~~   my friends   my mum

live	eat	love	like
in a house			

Present simple: affirmative

3 ☆ Circle the correct word.

1 I (love)/ cook my home. It's fantastic.
2 I **like** / **live** in a house next to the sea.
3 My mum and dad **love** / **work** in a restaurant at the beach.
4 They **cook** / **eat** pizzas and hamburgers for the people in the restaurant.
5 I **work** / **like** my mum's pizzas. They're very good.
6 I **eat** / **live** pizzas for lunch on Saturday and Sunday. Yum – my favourite!

4 ☆ Complete the sentences.

1 I like our teacher.
   Tara *likes* our teacher too.
2 My sister and I play the clarinet.
   My dad _____ the clarinet too.
3 Ewa and Silvia eat lunch at home.
   Toni _____ lunch at home too.
4 We live in London.
   Granddad _____ in London too.
5 I act in shows at school.
   My brother _____ in shows at school too.
6 I love chocolate cake.
   My dog _____ chocolate cake too.

5 ☆ Read and circle the correct word.

Hello. My name is Flip. I ¹**live** / **lives** in Snow York City and I ²**work** / **works** in a restaurant. We ³**cook** / **cooks** fantastic fish. Famous actors and singers ⁴**come** / **comes** to the restaurant. The actress Adelie Ping ⁵**eat** / **eats** lunch here. She ⁶**love** / **loves** our fish pasta. Her friends, the dancers Jan and Ant Arctic, ⁷**like** / **likes** our fish salads. The singer Rock Hopper ⁸**play** / **plays** the piano and ⁹**sing** / **sings** in the restaurant on Tuesdays. I ¹⁰**love** / **loves** his songs and he ¹¹**love** / **loves** our fish and chips!

6 ☆☆ Complete the sentences. Use the correct form of these verbs.

> play   live   ~~act~~   eat   work   love

1 Adelie Ping _**acts**_ in films.
2 She _____ in Snow York City.
3 Lots of actors and actresses _____ Flip's restaurant.
4 Jan and Ant Arctic _____ fish salad for lunch.
5 Rock Hopper _____ at Flip's restaurant on Tuesdays.
6 He _____ the piano.

7 ☆☆☆ Look at the information and write sentences in the present simple. Add the sticker.

1
Name: Sven and Glen Waddle
Job: saxophone players
Home: Ice Lake City
Favourite place: Flip's restaurant
Favourite food: fish sandwiches

2
Name: Penny Gwinn
Job: tennis player
Home: Snow York City
Favourite place: Flip's restaurant
Favourite food: fish and chips

> Sticker

1 *Sven and Glen Waddle play the saxophone. They live in Ice Lake City. They like Flip's restaurant and they love fish sandwiches.*
2 *Penny Gwinn* _____
_____

Puzzle Zone

8 Change one letter and make a new word. The pictures can help you.

1	2	3
wing	cake	fine
↓	↓	↓
sing	_____	_____
↓	↓	↓
song	_____	_____
↓	↓	↓
long	bike	love

School Food

Present simple: negative

1 ☆ **Complete the dialogue. Use *don't* or *doesn't*.**

Bish   I ¹*don't* like this snake.
Scrap It's OK, but I ²_____ like the salad.
Bish   My brother, Bosh, ³_____ eat salad but I love it.
Scrap Where's your brother now?
Bish   He's at home. He ⁴_____ eat his lunch at school. He ⁵_____ like school food. My granny, Mish and my granddad, Mash, ⁶_____ work. They cook my brother's favourite food at home.
Scrap Why are you at school for lunch?
Bish   I ⁷_____ like my granny and granddad's food!

2 ☆☆ **Look at the table and complete the sentences. Use the correct form of *like*.**

	Snake sandwiches	Dragon and salad	Bird's legs and chips
Bish	✗	✓	✗
Scrap	✓	✓	✓
Bosh	✓	✗	✗
Mish	✓	✗	✓
Mash	✗	✗	✓

1 Bosh *likes* snake sandwiches.
2 Bish and Bosh _____ bird's legs and chips.
3 Scrap _____ bird's legs and chips.
4 Bish _____ snake sandwiches.
5 Bish and Scrap _____ dragon and salad.
6 Bosh _____ dragon and salad.

3 ☆☆☆ **Write sentences about Mish and Mash.**

1 *Mish likes snake sandwiches.*
2 _____ .
3 _____ .
4 _____ .
5 _____ .

Reading

4 Read Sophie's paragraph. Add the sticker of her favourite food.

Four people work in the kitchen at our school. They cook our lunch, but six children in my class eat sandwiches from home. They have got lunchboxes. The hamburgers at school are very nice, and the chips are good too. My favourite food at school is pizza. We eat it on Fridays. My friends love pizza too. Today's lunch is chicken with apple and rice. Jenny loves it but I don't. Yuk!

Sticker

5 True or false? Correct the false sentences.

1 There isn't a kitchen at Sophie's school.
   False There is a kitchen at Jenny's school.

2 The people in the kitchen don't cook lunch.
   _____

3 Six children in Sophie's class eat food from home.
   _____

4 Sophie doesn't like chips.
   _____

5 Sophie and her friends eat hamburgers at school on Fridays.
   _____

6 Sophie likes chicken with apple and rice.
   _____

Talking Tips!

6 Complete the dialogue. Use these words.

What a pity   I'm sorry   Yum   Yuk
~~come and help~~   Come on

Mum   Matt, ^{1} **come and help** with the food.
Matt ^{2}_____, Mum, but I can't. I've got lots of homework today.
Mum ^{3}_____, Alex. Now!
Matt   Oh, OK. What's for lunch?
Mum   Pasta.
Alex ^{4}_____! I love pasta.
Mum   And there are apple cakes too.
Alex   Apple cakes? ^{5}_____! I don't like apple cakes.
Mum ^{6}_____!

Puzzle Zone

7 What is it? Circle the correct animal.

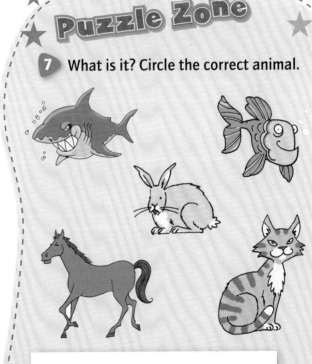

It lives in a house. It doesn't like rivers, lakes or seas. It doesn't eat salad. You can't ride it. It eats fish and chicken.

It's a _____.

Drinks

1 Circle the words for drinks.

2 Circle the odd word out and complete the reason. Then use the first letters of the circled words to answer the question. Add the sticker.

1 salad (pizza) apple juice   orange juice
   Pizza isn't cold.
2 tea   hot chocolate   coffee   apple juice
   _____ hot.
3 a hamburger   hot chocolate
   chocolate cake   salad
   _____ brown.
4 milk   tea   chicken   fish
   _____ from animals.
5 tea   milk   water   an apple
   _____ a drink.

What's Oscar and Jo-Jo's
favourite food?
p _ _ _ _ _

[Sticker]

Present simple: questions and short answers

3 ☆ Complete the questions and answers. Use *do, does, don't* or *doesn't*.

1 __*Do*__ you work in a café?

     Yes, I __*do*__ .

2 _____ you sing and dance there?

     No, I _____ .

3 _____ people drink tea in the café?

     Yes, they _____ .

4 _____ people eat fish and chips there?

     No, they _____ .

5 _____ your mum come to the café?

     Yes, she _____ .

6 _____ your mum like dogs?

     No, she _____ .

4 ☆☆ Write more questions for the waiter in Exercise 3. Then write his answers.

1 you / like / children ? ✗
   Do you like children?
   No, I don't.

2 your dad / work / in the café ? ✗
   _____
   _____

3 you / meet your friends / in the café ? ✓
   _____
   _____

4 your friends / drink / hot chocolate ? ✗
   _____
   _____

5 they / eat / chocolate cake ? ✓
   _____
   _____

Expressing likes and dislikes

5 Complete the dialogues. Use these sentences.

> They're OK   ~~Yes, they're fantastic~~ (x2)
> No, they're horrible

1 A Do you like computers?
   B *Yes, they're fantastic.* I love computers.
2 A Do you like computer games?
   B _____ . I've got one good game but lots of computer games are boring.
3 A Do you like my new pens?
   B _____ . They're beautiful colours.
4 A Do you like your sandwiches?
   B _____ . They've got fish in, and I don't like fish.

6 Complete the letters. Use these words.

> We   food   you   ~~café~~   drink
> do   don't   love   doesn't

Hi Billy,

We're in a ¹*café* today. ²_____ love the drinks, but we ³_____ like the waiter. He ⁴_____ like dogs. Do ⁵_____ like cafés? What's your favourite ⁶_____ ?

Love from

Jo-Jo

Hi Jo-Jo,

Yes, I ⁷_____ . I ⁸_____ cafés and restaurants. My favourite drink is water and my favourite ⁹_____ is fish.

Love from

Billy

Mr Big's Learning Blog

Watch out!

Lots of food words are the same in English and in your language – but the pronunciation is different.

Reading

1 Read and circle the correct answer.

1 Do people in Japan like fish? **Yes** / No
2 Do people in Japan drink tea with milk? Yes / No
3 Do people in Japan live a long time? Yes / No

FOOD IN MY COUNTRY

Hello. My name's Mika. I'm from Japan.

In my country, we eat lots of fish. *Sushi* is a famous food from Japan. It is rice with fish. We don't cook the fish, and we eat the *sushi* cold. Our favourite drink is green tea. We drink it every day. In Britain, they drink tea with milk, but we don't like milk in our tea in Japan.

The food in Japan is very healthy and people here live a long time. My mum's granny and granddad are ninety-nine, and lots of their friends are a hundred!

2 Read the text again and complete Mika's answers in the table.

		Mika	You
1	Where are you from?	*Japan*	
2	What's the name of a famous food from your country?		
3	What is it?	*rice with fish*	
4	What is the favourite drink in your country?		
5	Is the food in your country healthy?		

Writing

3 Complete the table in Exercise 2 for you.

4 Write a paragraph. Use the information in the table.

Food in my country
I'm from …
_____
_____
_____
_____

Summer Fun

My Picture Dictionary

The beach

1 Complete the words.

1 t <u>o w e</u> l

5 b __ __ t

2 s __ __

6 i __ __ c __ __ __ m

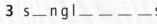

3 s __ n g l __ __ __ __ __ s

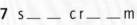

7 s __ __ c r __ __ m

4 p __ __ n __ __

8 u __ b r __ __ __ a

2 Complete the puzzle.

1 These are for your eyes in the sun.

2 You can eat this lunch at the beach or the park.

3 This food is very cold – yum!

4 You can go fast on the water in this.

5 It's nice under this. It isn't hot.

6 This is yellow and very hot.

7 This is for the beach and the bathroom.

8 This is for your body in the sun.

¹S
U
N
G
L
A
S
S
E
⁸S

my words

What is in your beach bag? Write the things here.

_____ _____ _____

What are your favourite things at the beach?

_____ _____ _____

Discover **5** extra words. Go to page 71.

The Swimming Pool

Imperatives

1 ☆ **Where? Write A or B. Then circle the imperative.**

A At the beach
B In your English class

1 (Don't write) on the walls.
2 Don't drink the sea water.
3 Don't swim under the boats.
4 Listen to your teacher.
5 Don't play football next to the picnic.
6 Speak in English.
7 Don't eat in the classroom.

2 ☆ **Order the sentences.**

1 the pool | eat | next to | Don't | ice cream .
Don't eat ice cream next to the pool.

2 Wear | hot days | suncream | on .
_____

3 splash | Don't | in the pool .
_____

4 Drink | from the café | water .
_____

5 the baby pool | in | Don't | dive .
_____

6 swim | Don't | here .
_____

3 ☆☆ **Look at the pictures. Write the imperatives.**

1 ✗ (play) *Don't play music.*

2 ✗ (play) _____ .

3 ✓ (wear) _____ .

4 ✗ (eat) _____ .

5 ✓ (wear) _____ .

4 ☆☆ **All the sentences on the sign are wrong. Write the correct sign.**

1 **Don't come to the Pool Café!**
2 **Don't eat our fantastic sandwiches!**
3 **Don't drink our hot and cold drinks!**
4 **Come here with dogs!**
5 **Eat your picnics here!**
6 **Write on the tables!**

1 *Come to the Pool Café!*
2 _____
3 _____
4 _____
5 _____
6 _____

5 ☆☆☆ **Write a sign for a music class. Use the imperatives of some of these verbs.**

listen | phone | play | sing
drink | eat | write | dance

1 _____
_____
2 _____
_____
3 _____
_____
4 _____
_____

Clothes

6 Complete the sentences. Use these words.

> shorts   T-shirt   dress   trousers
> swimsuit   ~~hat~~   shoes

1 I like your new 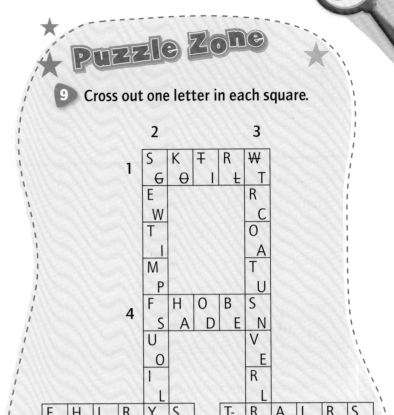 _**hat**_ .

2 Your _____ are nice.

3 Is that Charlotte's _____ ?

4 Look at those horrible _____ .

5 That's a cool _____ .

6 Don't wear those _____ !

7 I love this _____ .

7 Complete. Use *is* or *are*. Add the sticker.

My hat [1] _**is**_ white and yellow.
My dress [2] _____ green and blue.
My shorts [3] _____ black and orange.
My shoes [4] _____
  orange too.
My trousers [5] _____
  fantastic.
They're very small and
  red.
But people do not like me
With trousers on my head.

| Sticker |

8 Write true sentences. Use words from Exercise 5.

1 On a hot day I wear _**a hat, shorts and a T-shirt.**_
  _____

2 At the swimming pool I wear _____
  _____ .

3 On my feet I wear _____ .
  _____

4 At school I wear _____ .
  _____

Puzzle Zone

9 Cross out one letter in each square.

	2		3	
1	S ~~K~~	~~T~~ R	~~W~~ R	
	~~G~~	~~O~~ I	~~Ł~~ T	
	E		R	
	W		C	
	T		O	
	I		A	
	M		T	
	P		U	
4	F	H O	B S	
	S	A D	E N	
	U		V	
	O		E	
	I		R	
	L		L	

5	E H	I R	Y S	6	T- R	A I	R S
	S W	O M	T K		G- S	H P	U T

10 Find six clothes words.

1 _____   4 _____
2 _____   5 _____
3 _____   6 _____

Talking Tips!

11 Complete the dialogue. Use these words.

> Me too   ~~Really~~   Hi, guys   Yum

Jenny   Look, Sophie. Matt's at the pool too!
Sophie   [1] _**Really?**_ Where?
Jenny   There, on the green towel. Hi, Matt!
Matt   Oh! [2] _____ ! Who are you with today?
Sophie   My mum.
Jenny   We've got a big picnic. There are lots of cheese sandwiches.
Matt   [3] _____ ! I love cheese, and I'm very hungry.
Sophie   [4] _____ ! Let's eat our lunch now.

Verb review

1 ☆ Match the sentence halves.

1 Dexter   a   a swimming pool at the park.
2 There   b   like the crocodile in the lake.
3 He doesn't   c   is at the Adventure Park.
4 He's   d   are lots of people at the park.
5 There's   e   football today.
6 He can't play   f   got new sunglasses.

2 ☆ Circle the correct words.

1 Dexter **has got** / **have got** a bag.
2 Dexter **can** / **am** ride the horses at the Adventure Park.
3 The people on the horses **is** / **are** sad.
4 There **is** / **are** a girl with a big rabbit.
5 People **can** / **eat** fish and chips at the café.
6 The waiters at the café **wear** / **wears** big hats.
7 Dexter **like** / **likes** his drink.

3 ☆☆ Look at the pictures of Dexter at the Adventure Park. Are the sentences in Exercise 2 true or false? Correct the false sentences.

1 *false   Dexter hasn't got a bag.*
He's got a camera.

2 _____
_____
3 _____
_____
4 _____
_____
5 _____
_____
6 _____
_____
7 _____
_____

4 ⭐⭐ **Complete the text. Use these words.**

> likes   can   has got   ~~is~~   love   eat   There's   comes

Hello. My name's Freya. My favourite place for summer fun ¹*is* the river in my village. My friends and I ²_____ it. It ³_____ very cold water, but you ⁴_____ swim in it on hot days. ⁵_____ a small park next to the river. We ⁶_____ picnics there. My dog ⁷_____ too. He ⁸_____ the cold water.

5 ⭐⭐ **There are three adventure parks near Freya's home.**
Complete the sentences with a suitable word or words.

	Coasterpark	Wackyland	Thrill World
lakes	1	2	0
boats	no	yes	no
horses	yes	no	yes
cafés	1	3	1
swimming pools	0	1	2
Freya says:	boring	fantastic	fantastic

1 *There are* two lakes at Wackyland.
2 You _____ go in boats at Coasterpark.
3 You _____ ride horses at Thrill World.
4 Coasterpark and Thrill World _____ one café.
5 Coasterpark _____ a swimming pool.
6 Freya _____ like Coasterpark.
7 Wackyland and Thrill World _____ fantastic.

6 ⭐⭐⭐ **Write four more sentences about the adventure parks in Exercise 5.**

1 _____   3 _____
2 _____   4 _____

⭐ Puzzle Zone ⭐

7 **Where is Freya today? Write letter 1 of these words and make a sentence. Add the sticker.**

      Sticker

S __ __ __ __ __

__ __ __ __ __ __ __ __ .

Question review

1 ☆ Order the questions.

1 this is Billy's party ?
Is this Billy's party?
2 Billy's friends you are ?
_____
3 live under the sea you do ?
_____

4 dance can the basketball players ?
_____
5 got you a drink have ?
_____
6 there food is at the party ?
_____

2 ☆ Complete the questions with these words. Then complete the answers.

Has Is ~~Does~~ Can Is Does

1 *Does* Billy like parties?
Yes, *he does* .
2 _____ he a hamster?
No, _____ .
3 _____ he got eight legs?
Yes, _____ .
4 _____ he live in the mountains?
No, _____ .
5 _____ he dance?
Yes, _____ .
6 _____ there a dragon at his party?
No, _____ .

3 ☆ Match the answers with the questions in Exercise 1.

a Yes, we are.   2
b No, I don't.   ___
c Yes, it is.   ___

d Yes, I have.   ___
e No, they can't.   ___
f Yes, there is.   ___

4 ☆☆ Complete the questions. Whose are the answers? Add the sticker.

1 *Do you like* animals?
Yes, I do.
2 _____ a waiter?
No, I'm not.
3 _____ basketball?
No, I can't.
4 _____ three heads?
Yes, I have.
5 _____ in a shop?
Yes, I do.
6 _____ pets in your shop?
Yes, there are.

Sticker

Telling the time

5 Complete the dialogue. Use these words.

o'clock   half   past   ~~party~~   time   at

A Can you go to the ¹ ___party___ today?
B What party?
A Billy's party. It's at six ² _____ .
B What ³ _____ is it now?
A It's ⁴ _____ past three.
B Well, I've got a dance class ⁵ _____
   half ⁶ _____ four, but I can go to
   Billy's party too.
A Great!

6 Write the times.

1 ___It's one o'clock.___   2 _____

3 _____   4 _____

5 _____   6 _____

Puzzle Zone

7 Find the clocks and colour the squares.
What letters do you see? Complete the
sentence with the letters.

1 eight o'clock   7 four o'clock
2 half past twelve   8 nine o'clock
3 five o'clock   9 half past two
4 half past nine   10 half past four
5 half past ten   11 one o'clock
6 eleven o'clock   12 half past eight

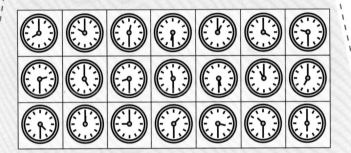

On very hot days and very cold days, wear
a _ a _ .

Mr Big's Learning Blog

Remember old words

Your vocabulary notebook
isn't only for new words. Don't
forget the old words! Look again at
your words from the start of the year.

Let's Revise!

Vocabulary

1 Vocabulary race! Write as many words as you can in one minute.

Food	Drinks	Clothes	At the beach	Verbs
pizza chicken				

(½ point per word)   __ /10

Grammar

2 Write negative sentences. Use the words in brackets.

1 We like ice cream. (cake)
   We don't like cake.

2 Go to the beach. (swimming pool)
   _____

3 There's a red boat in the sea. (a green boat)
   _____

4 You can swim. (dive)
   _____

5 He's got new sunglasses. (shoes)
   _____

6 She lives in Italy. (Greece)
   _____

7 I'm a dancer. (singer)
   _____

                                   __ /12

3 Write the questions and answers.

1 he / hot ? ✓   _Is he hot?_   _Yes, he is._

2 you / got / a swimsuit ? ✗
   _____
   _____

3 he / like / picnics ? ✗
   _____
   _____

4 there / lots of people / at the beach ? ✓
   _____
   _____

5 she / can / play / tennis ? ✗
   _____
   _____

6 they / work / on that boat ? ✓
   _____
   _____

                                   __ /10

Functions

4 Order the questions. Complete three different answers for each question.

1   time   what   it   is   ?
   _____
   a It's _____ .
   b It's _____ .
   c It's _____ .

2   you   those shorts   like   do   ?
   _____
   a Yes, they're _____ .
   b They're _____ .
   c No, they're _____ .

                                   __ /8

Your score	Your total score
	__ /40
😃 30–40 😊 20–30 😣 0–20	

Extra Words

Unit 1

1 Complete the sentences. Use these words.

> cake ~~garden~~ party card camera

1 This **_garden_** is very big and green.
2 This is a cool photo. Your **c**_____ is great.
3 The chocolate **c**_____ is from my mum.
4 It's my birthday. Come to my **p**_____ .
5 Look at the picture on my birthday **c**_____ .

Unit 2

2 Complete the sentences. Use these words.

> Africa ~~Asia~~ North America
> South America Europe

1 China is in **_Asia_** .
2 Poland is in _____ .
3 The USA is in _____ .
4 Argentina is in _____ .
5 Egypt is in _____ .

Unit 3

3 Circle the words. Match them with the pictures.

1 frisbee
2 teddy bear
3 bat
4 mask
5 hat

Unit 4

4 Look at the picture on page 39 of the Student Book. Match.

1 bandage   a the fish
2 cage   b the bird
3 basket   c the dog and the cat
4 collar   d the cat
5 bowl   e the dog

Unit 5

5 Where are they? Match the words.

1 teacher   a wall
2 clock   b wall
3 board   c classroom
4 light   d wall
5 cupboard   e ceiling

Unit 6

6 Match the words with the pictures.

> climb a tree _3_ run rollerblade paint jump

Unit 7

7 Look at the picture on page 69 of the Student Book. Complete the sentences with these words.

> plate ~~knife~~ glass fork jug

1 There's a **_knife_** and _____ in her hands.
2 There's water in the man's _____ .
3 There is a hamburger on the man's _____ .
4 She has got a big _____ on her table.

Unit 8

8 Match the words with the pictures.

> sand _3_ shell rocks crab waves

Pearson Education Limited
Edinburgh Gate
Harlow
Essex CM20 2JE
England

and Associated Companies throughout the world.

www.pearsonelt.com

© Pearson Education Limited 2010

First published 2009

Twenty Third impression 2024

Set in 12/15pt ATQuay Sans Book and 12/15pt ATQuay Medium

Printed in Slovakia by Neografia

ISBN 978-1-4058-6651-4

Authors' acknowledgements
The author would like to thank the Discover English team for
their support, expertise and dedication. With special thanks to:
Jo Pearson, Sue Jones, Nicola Sugden, Jo Stevenson, Andrew
Oliver, Heather Lane, Yvette Stewart.

Fiona would also like to acknowledge Krysianna and Andreas for
their patience, good humour and understanding.

Illustrated by Andrew Hennessey: 4br, 5cr, 14tr, 33, 40t, 44bl,
56t, 57, 63, 64, 71br, 73; Andy Peters 9br, 18, 26t, 31t, 48br,
73; Gary Wing 10t, 25b, 35, 62r, 73; Julian Mosedale 44t; Mark
Ruffle 39, 65tl; Moreno Chicchiera 5l, 7, 9tl, 21cl, 23, 24, 32, 42b,
43b, 57t, 58tr, 60tr, 61r, 67b 73; Paul Daviz 49tl & tr; Piers Baker
6cr, 7, 12, 13, 20, 28l, 29, 36tl, 37, 45, 49br, 52b, 53l & r, 59br,
60tr, 61r, 68t, 69br, 73; Rob Davis 15, 16, 21tr, 48l, 51, 53br, 69bl,
71bl & cr, 73; Sean Longcroft 20bl, 34t, 41b, 47, 55c, 66r.

Photo Acknowledgements
The publisher would like to thank the following for their kind
permission to reproduce their photographs:

(Key: b-bottom; c-centre; l-left; r-right; t-top)

Martin Beddall: 2, 3l, 3r, 8 (1), 8 (2), 8 (3), 8 (4), 8 (5), 8 (6), 8tr,
11, 17, 25, 27, 50, 59; John Birdsall Social Issues Photo Library:
Clare Marsh 8br; Rex Features: F.Webster 37; Hayley Madden 49;
Mangiarotti 46r; Matt Baron/BEI 19; Mercury Press Agency 46l

All other images © Pearson Education

Picture Research by: Louise Edgeworth

La presente publicación se ajusta a la cartografía oficial
establecida por el Poder Ejecutivo Nacional de la República
Argentina a través del IGN-Ley 22.923 y fue aprobada por
Expte. N° GG09 2001/5 de noviembre de 2009.

Stickers

Unit 0
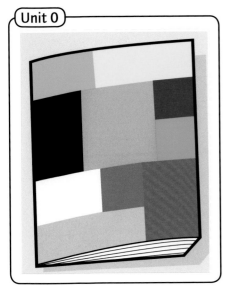

Unit 1

Unit 2

Unit 3

Unit 4

Unit 5

Unit 6

Unit 7

Unit 8